When I'm At Work

Paramedic

Written by Sue Barraclough
Photography by Chris Fairclough

W
FRANKLIN WATTS
LONDON • SYDNEY

This edition published 2011
Franklin Watts
338 Euston Road, London NW1 3BH

Franklin Watts Australia
Level 17/207 Kent Street, Sydney NSW 2000

Editors: Caryn Jenner, Sarah Ridley
Designer: Jemima Lumley
Art direction: Jonathan Hair
Photography: Chris Fairclough

The publisher wishes to thank Simon, Julie and Heather of the West Midlands
Ambulance Service for all their help with this book. Many thanks also to
Simeon and St Luke's Church of England Primary School, Blakenhall.

Photograph page 29 reproduced by kind permission of the West Midlands
Ambulance Service.

A CIP catalogue record for this book is available
from the British Library

ISBN 978 1 4451 0700 4

Dewey decimal classification number: 362.18

Printed in China

Franklin Watts is a division of Hachette Children's Books,
an Hachette UK company. www.hachette.co.uk

Loans are up to 28 days. Fines are charged if items are not returned by the due date. Items can be renewed at the Library, via the internet or by telephone up to 3 times. Items in demand will not be renewed.

Please use a bookmark

Date for return		
FRANKLEY LIBRARY FRANKLEY COMMUNITY HIGH SCHOOL NEW STREET, FRANKLEY BIRMINGHAM B45 0EU Telephone: 0121 464 7676 NR		

Check out our online catalogue to see what's in stock, or to renew or reserve books.

www.birmingham.gov.uk/libcat

www.birmingham.gov.uk/libraries

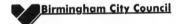 **Birmingham City Council**

B **Birmingham Libraries**

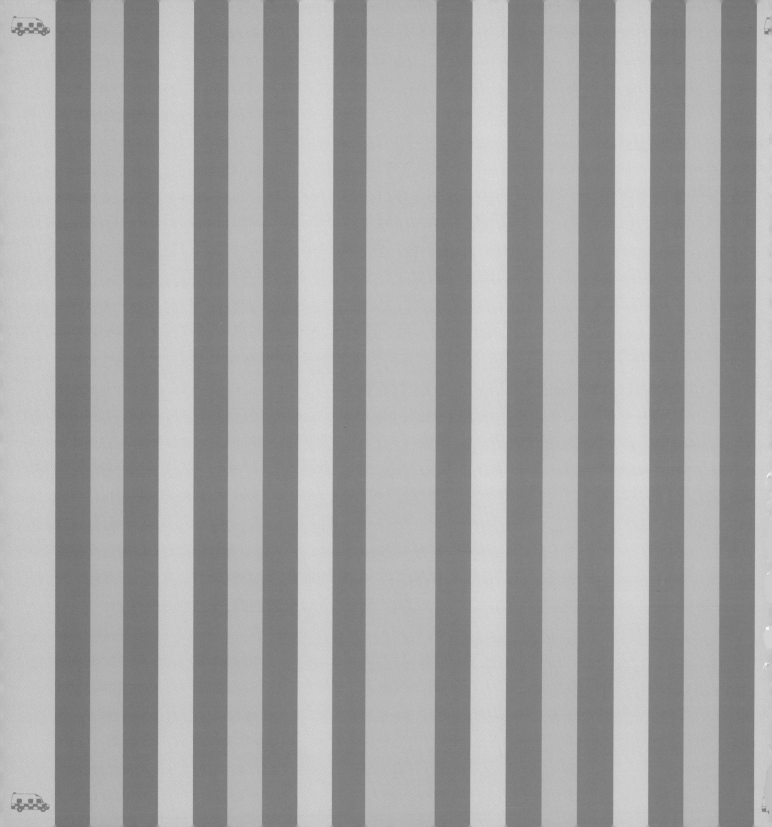

Contents

I am a paramedic 6

Checking the equipment 8

Emergency call-out 10

Racing to the emergency 12

A bicycle accident 14

Going to hospital 16

Answering another call 18

A school visit 20

Exploring the ambulance 22

At the end of the day 24

Emergency equipment 26

Keeping safe and calling 999 28

Glossary and index 30

I am a paramedic

My name is Simon and I am based at an ambulance station in Wolverhampton. Paramedics spend most of their time answering emergency calls.

I work with Julie who drives the ambulance. Like me, Julie is trained to give emergency medical help. But I have also been trained to give life-saving medicines.

Checking the equipment

The ambulance is full of equipment to help people who are sick or injured. We check all the equipment when we start work.

I also carry a green bag which contains medicines and other equipment.

Emergency call-out

If there is an accident, the 999 call is put through to our control centre.

The control centre calls us with details of the emergency. We hurry out to the ambulance.

Racing to the emergency

As we set off, machines inside the ambulance give us more information about what has happened and how to get to the accident.

Julie turns on the lights and the siren. We need to get to the accident as fast as we can.

A bicycle accident

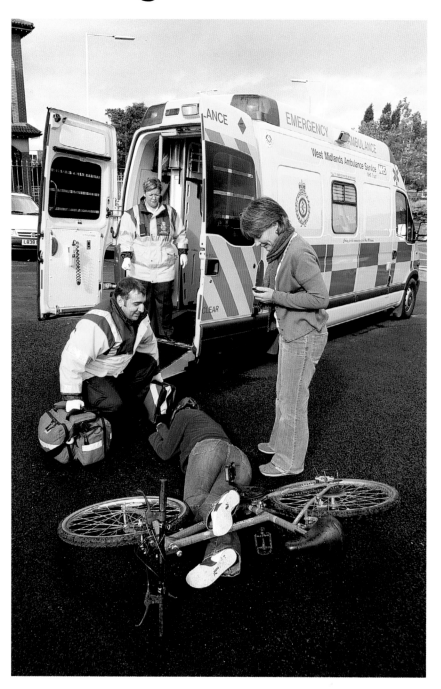

As soon as we arrive, I find out the cyclist's name. Heather says that her leg is hurt.

I put a blanket over Heather to keep her warm and Julie fetches a splint.

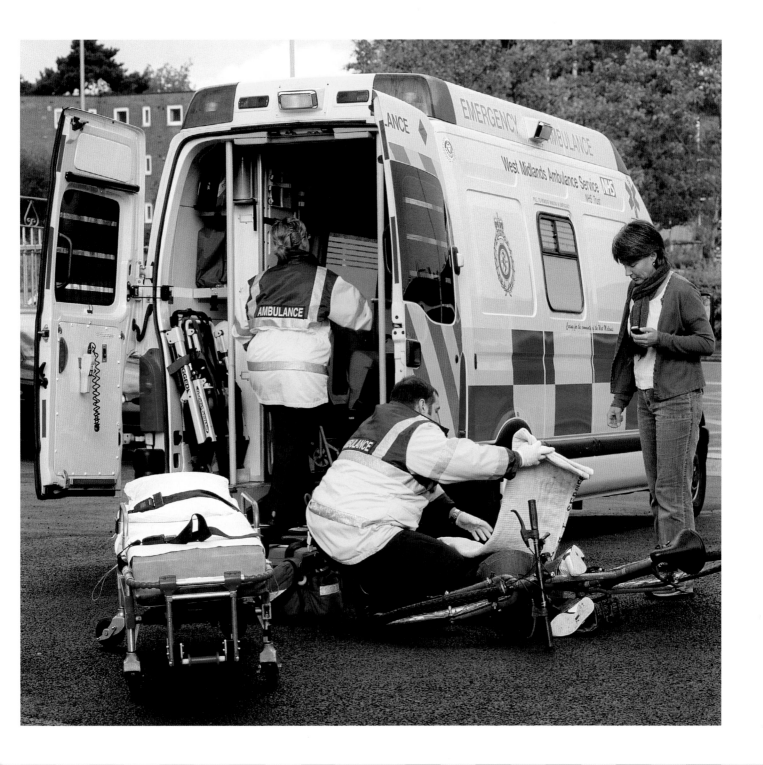

Going to hospital

I have put the splint on Heather's injured leg to protect it. Her helmet has protected her head. I get into the ambulance with Heather.

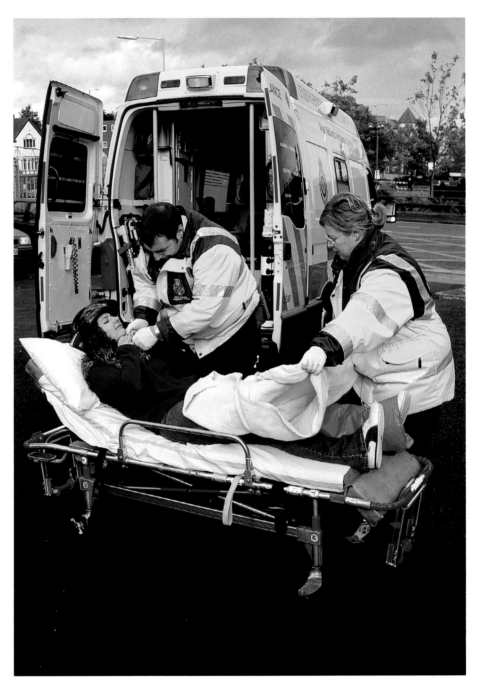

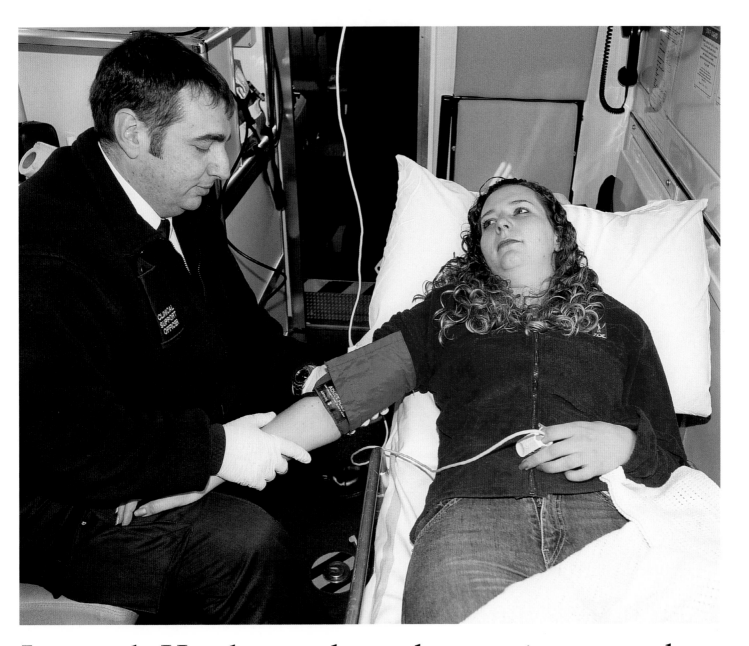

I sit with Heather and use the monitor to make some health checks as we set off for the hospital.

Answering another call

We are often called to another emergency on our way back to the ambulance station.

Simeon has fallen from a climbing frame and injured his arm.

I think Simeon's arm may be broken, so I put the arm in a sling. We help Simeon to get up so we can take him to hospital by ambulance.

A school visit

Sometimes I go into schools to talk to children about my job. We show them some of the equipment that we use. And I talk to the children about calling 999 for help.

Exploring the ambulance

This class is going to have a look around our ambulance.

I show them where things are stored and how they work.

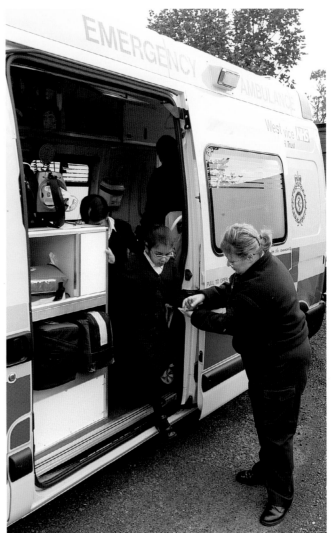

At the end of the day

Back at the ambulance station I use the computer to do my paperwork. I write reports about what has happened.

Before I finish work, another paramedic team arrives. I sign the ambulance over to them. Then I can go home.

Emergency equipment

A **paramedic's bag** holds first-aid equipment and life-saving medicines.

A **splint** will keep a leg still and supported if it is injured or broken.

A **monitor** is a machine that gives the paramedic information about a patient's breathing, blood pressure and heart rate.

The **first-aid kit** has bandages, cotton wool, wipes, plasters and other useful items.

Ambulance is written back-to-front on the front of the vehicle so that car drivers can read it in their car mirrors.

Paramedics wear **latex gloves** to treat someone. This is to avoid spreading or catching germs.

Keeping safe and calling 999

- Always wear a seat belt in a car or coach.
- Take care when you cross the road – STOP, LOOK AND LISTEN before you cross a road.
- Always wear a helmet when you ride your bicycle.
- Never play near roads, water or railways.
- Be aware and take care of younger children as you play.
- Take extra care when playing on a climbing frame.

In an emergency

Stay calm

Call 999

Give the operator your phone number and the address.

Describe what has happened.

If you call 999 you will be put through to a control centre like this one. They will ask you what has happened. This is so they can decide what sort of vehicle to send. Stay on the phone and answer any other questions. The ambulance will be on its way.

Glossary and index

ambulance station - the buildings where the ambulances are kept, and where paramedics wait to be called out. **Pages 6, 18, 25**

call-out - the telephone message that asks for an ambulance to be sent out. **Page 10**

control centre - the building where all the 999 calls are answered. **Pages 10, 29**

first-aid - treatment given before seeing a doctor. **Pages 26, 27**

health check - tests to find out how well the body is working. **Page 17**

latex - thin stretchy rubber. **Page 27**

medicine - pills and liquids given to people to help them get better. **Pages 7, 9, 26**

report - written record of what happened that day. **Page 25**

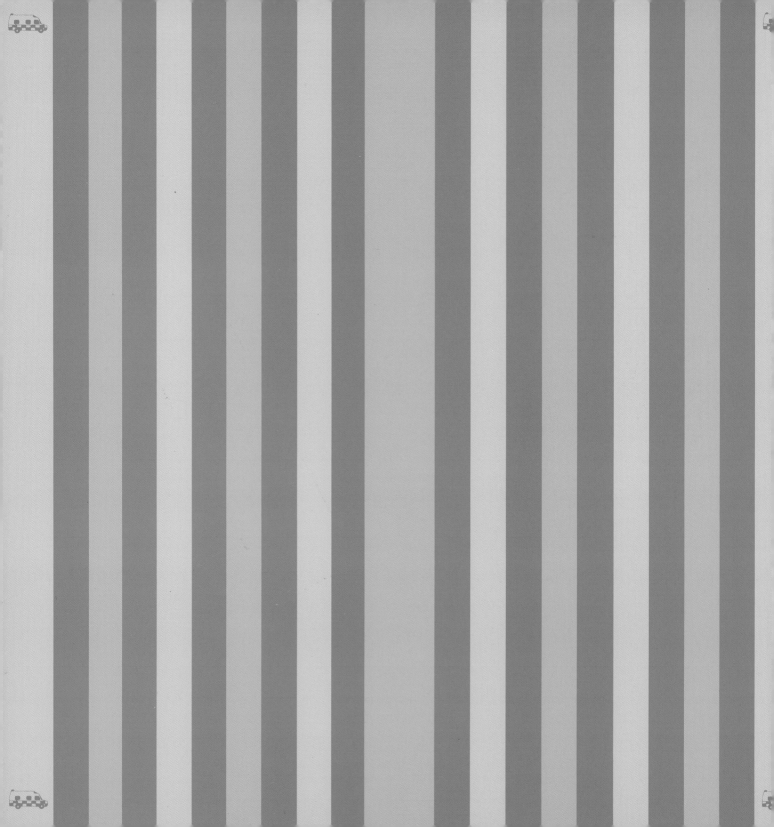